INVASIVE SPECIES

ASIAN GIANT HORNETS

by Alicia Z. Klepeis

pogo

Ideas for Parents and Teachers

Pogo Books let children practice reading informational text while introducing them to nonfiction features such as headings, labels, sidebars, maps, and diagrams, as well as a table of contents, glossary, and index.

Carefully leveled text with a strong photo match offers early fluent readers the support they need to succeed.

Before Reading

- "Walk" through the book and point out the various nonfiction features. Ask the student what purpose each feature serves.
- Look at the glossary together. Read and discuss the words.

Read the Book

- Have the child read the book independently.
- Invite him or her to list questions that arise from reading.

After Reading

- Discuss the child's questions. Talk about how he or she might find answers to those questions.
- Prompt the child to think more. Ask: Asian giant hornets and honeybees both have stripes and stingers. How else are they similar? How are they different?

Pogo Books are published by Jump!
5357 Penn Avenue South
Minneapolis, MN 55419
www.jumplibrary.com

Library of Congress Cataloging-in-Publication Data

Names: Klepeis, Alicia, 1971- author.
Title: Asian giant hornets / by Alicia Z. Klepeis.
Description: Minneapolis, MN: Jump!, Inc., [2023]
Series: Invasive species | Includes index.
Audience: Ages 7-10
Identifiers: LCCN 2021055120 (print)
LCCN 2021055121 (ebook)
ISBN 9781636907833 (hardcover)
ISBN 9781636907840 (paperback)
ISBN 9781636907857 (ebook)
Subjects: LCSH: Hornets–Juvenile literature.
Introduced insects–Juvenile literature.
Classification: LCC QL568.V5 K54 2023 (print) | LCC
QL568.V5 (ebook) | DDC 595.79/8–dc23/eng/20211110
LC record available at https://lccn.loc.gov/2021055120
LC ebook record available at https://lccn.loc.
gov/2021055121

Editor: Eliza Leahy
Designer: Michelle Sonnek

Photo Credits: kojihirano/iStock, cover, 3, 4 (hornet); yasuo inoue/Shutterstock, 1; HHelene/Shutterstock, 4 (honeybee); Phil Degginger/Alamy, 5, 23; David Hansche/iStock, 6-7; Mayumi.K.Photography/Shutterstock, 8; Danita Delimont/Shutterstock, 9; QueSeraSera/Shutterstock, 10-11; Satoshi Kuribayashi/Minden Pictures, 12-13; Steve Downeranth/SuperStock, 14-15; 22 TREE HOUSE/Shutterstock, 16-17; contrail1/iStock, 18 (hornets); Shutterstock, 18 (pesticide); Karen Ducey/Getty Images, 19; kororokerokero/iStock, 20-21.

Printed in the United States of America at
Corporate Graphics in North Mankato, Minnesota.

TABLE OF CONTENTS

CHAPTER 1

BIGGER THAN BEES

What insect looks like a European honeybee but weighs 20 times more? It is an Asian giant hornet!

This hornet is colorful. Its head is orange or yellow. It has big, black eyes. Its body has black and orange or yellow stripes.

Each hornet has two **antennas**. They also have two sets of wings. Their wings help them fly up to 25 miles (40 kilometers) per hour!

TAKE A LOOK!

What are the body parts of an Asian giant hornet? Take a look!

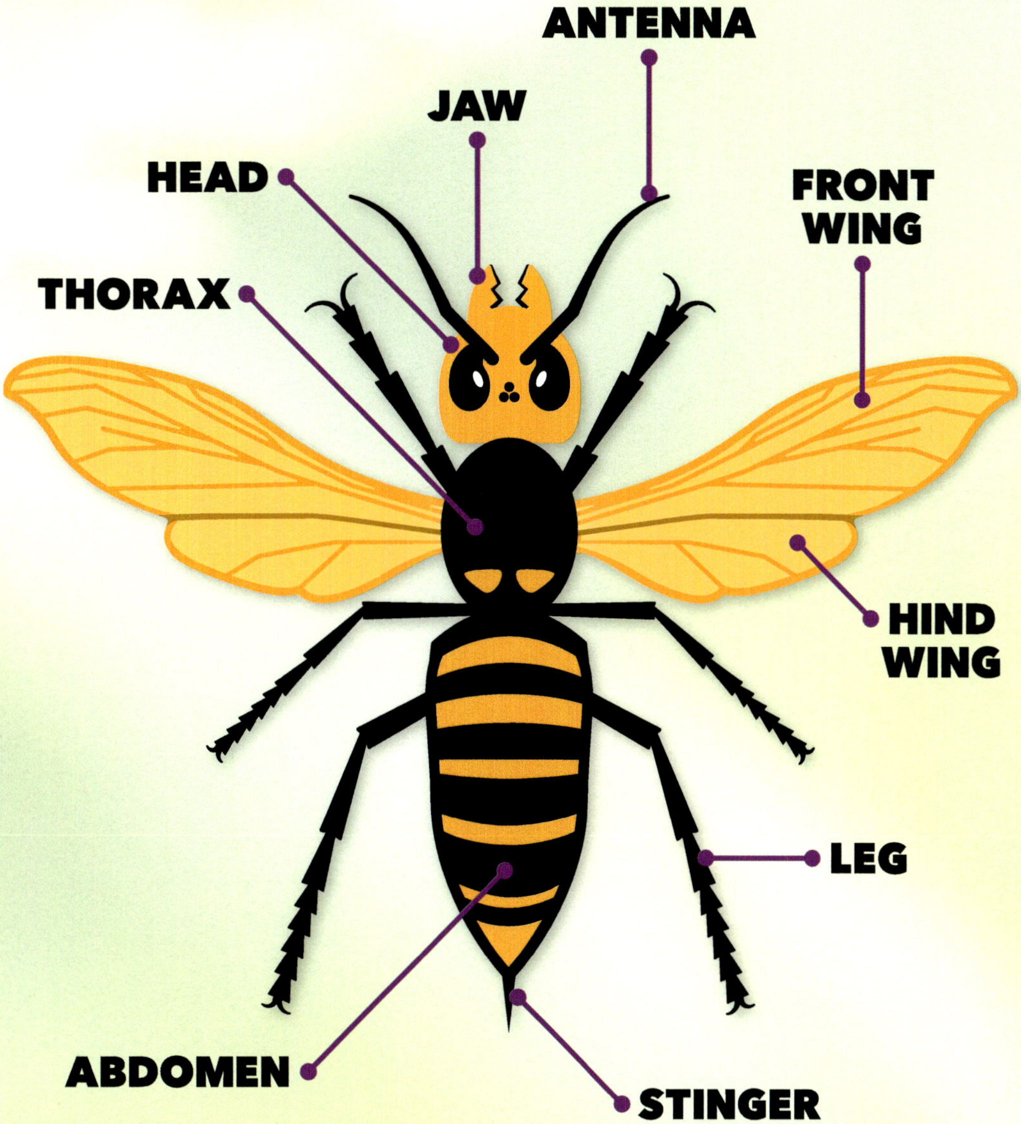

CHAPTER 2

LOOK OUT, BEES!

Asian giant hornets are **native** to Asia. They live in Asia's forests and low mountains.

In 2019, they were first seen in forests in Canada and Washington. How did they get to North America? Scientists are not sure. They may have come on a ship from Asia.

Asian giant hornets are an **invasive species** in North America. They harm their new **environments**. How? They eat European honeybees. They often hunt alone. But sometimes they work together to attack a beehive. A small group can kill 30,000 honeybees in just a few hours.

TAKE A LOOK!

Where have Asian giant hornets been found in North America? Where do scientists think they could spread next? Take a look!

Like honeybees, Asian giant hornets live in **colonies**. They work together to build nests. These are usually underground. They also work together to raise their young. **Larvae** hatch from eggs. Adults bring food to larvae in the nest. They often bring them bees they have killed.

DID YOU KNOW?

One colony can have hundreds of Asian giant hornets.

larva

Japanese honeybees
Asian giant hornet

In Asia, if a hornet comes into a Japanese honeybee hive, the colony surrounds it. This is called a bee ball. They flap their wings. This raises the temperature. The heat kills the hornet.

In North America, European honeybees don't make bee balls. They try to sting the hornets. But their stings aren't enough. The hornets easily take over.

DID YOU KNOW?

Honeybees can only sting once. Asian giant hornets can sting many times. They also have more **venom**.

European honeybees were dying off in North America before Asian giant hornets arrived. Why? **Pesticides** and **pollution** are two causes. The hornets put these bees in even more danger.

European honeybees are **pollinators**. We need them to grow **crops**. They also make honey.

pollen

CHAPTER 3

TIME TO ACT

Scientists are working to stop the spread of Asian giant hornets in North America. They find their nests. Then they use fire or pesticides to destroy the nests and kill the hornets.

People make traps. The hornets get stuck inside and die.

Asian giant hornets are amazing insects. But North America is not their natural home.

We can all help stop the spread of invasive species. Learn about the insects that live in your area. Grow native plants. The honeybees will thank you!

DID YOU KNOW?

Asian giant hornets are also called sparrow hornets. Some people call them murder hornets. But hornets don't look for people to sting.

ACTIVITIES & TOOLS

TRY THIS!

BUILD A BEE POND

Help honeybees by building a bee pond in this fun activity!

What You Need:

- plant pot
- shallow pan or dish
- pebbles or rocks
- water
- pencil
- notebook

1. **Choose an outdoor space that has some shade.**
2. **Place the plant pot upside down on the ground.**
3. **Set the pan or dish on top of the pot.**
4. **Put pebbles or rocks in the pan or dish.**
5. **Pour in just enough water so the tops of the pebbles or rocks stick out above the water's surface.**
6. **Change the water each day. Observe the bees that visit. What do they do? Record your observations in your notebook.**

GLOSSARY

antennas: Feelers on the heads of insects.

colonies: Groups of hornets or bees that live together.

crops: Plants that are grown as food.

environments: The natural surroundings of living things.

invasive species: Any kind of living organism that is not native to a specific area.

larvae: Insects in the stage of development between eggs and pupae.

native: Growing or living naturally in a particular area of the world.

pesticides: Chemicals used to kill pests, such as insects.

pollinators: Insects or animals that pollinate flowers, allowing them to reproduce.

pollution: Harmful materials that damage or contaminate the air, water, and soil.

venom: Poison produced by some animals, usually passed into a victim's body by a bite or sting.

INDEX

TO LEARN MORE

Finding more information is as easy as 1, 2, 3.

1. Go to www.factsurfer.com
2. Enter "Asiangianthornets" into the search box.
3. Choose your book to see a list of websites.

FACT SURFER